20
TATTED
MOTIFS

by

Rosemarie
Peel

Contents

Other tatting books
from Lacet Publications:
TAT FIVE
YULETIDE TATTING
BEAD TATTING

ISBN 1 874688 04 4

Printed in England by
Printhaus Graphique Ltd
Northampton.

First published in December 1993 by
LACET PUBLICATIONS
29 St Nicolas Park Drive, Nuneaton, CV11 6DL,
ENGLAND

Introduction

This book is very much a starting point for greater things. Most of the patterns are individual motifs which can be used on their own in small mounts or grouped together in arrangements. Some ideas have been illustrated for you on the front and back cover and on pages 9 and 14 but you will be sure to come up with your own collections.

Threads are not specified as any tatting threads can be used. The only restraint I suggest would be to use all the same thickness and quality of thread in an arrangement, for uniformity.

Please experiment with colour, the possibilities for unique designs are endless with so many coloured and variegated threads on the market.

Split rings

A split ring is very useful for getting along the work without having extra ends. For example, it can take the work on from a central ring of a motif to the first row, or from one row to the next, or along a line of rings without having to leave a length of thread each time.

The ball thread needs to be on a second shuttle. Take the thread of Sh1 round your hand to make a ring in the normal way. Make the ds as stated for the first shuttle to complete the first half of the ring. Put Sh1 down and pick up Sh2 keeping the ring on your hand. The second shuttle will work up the other side of the ring, in the space between your first and little finger, in a slightly different manner. The right hand movements for making the ds are the same as usual but the thread in the ring is not allowed to reverse. It must be kept tight and the ds are pulled up on it as if you were sewing blanket stitches (Quote: 'It feels odd').

After completing the ds as stated for Sh2, put it down and take up Sh1 to close the ring. The two threads are now in position to go on and make another split ring or to continue the pattern with ordinary chains and rings.

A row of eight split rings:
(split ring Sh1, 8 Sh2, 8 close) 8 times

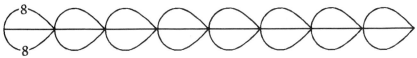

Abbreviations

TATTING TERM and ABBREVIATION		EXPLANATION	DIAGRAM SYMBOLS
Double stitch	1, ds	The number denotes the quantity. Made up of two halves, plain and purl.	
Picot	-	Comes between whole ds. - (regular) - - (long)	
Chain	Ch	A number of ds. made with the ball thread and sitting on the shuttle thread.	
Ring	R	A number of ds. made using shuttle thread only.	
Close ring	close	Work continues from this close-up point on the ring.	
Reverse work	RW	The ring is tipped upside down before the next chain is made. Another RW tips it back.	
Shuttle	Sh	Combinations of these symbols are used with every pattern to indicate what is needed.	
Ball			
Join	+	A join is made to the appropriate free picot followed by a purl. This counts as the next ds.	
Lock join	LJ	Make this join with the shuttle thread in use at the time.	
Josephine knot	JK	The number denotes how many half stitches to make.	
Split ring		See page 3.	

Polyanthus

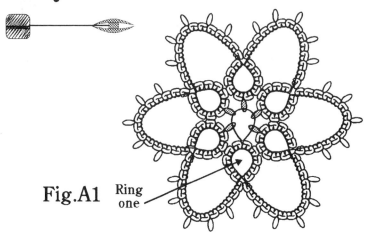

Fig.A1 Ring one

Fig.A1
Make the picot of Ring one large enough to accommodate the
five picots which will be joined to it.
Ring one 5 - - 5 close, RW,
(Ch 3 - 2 - 2 - 2 - 2 - 3, RW, R 5 + 5 close, RW,) 5 times,
Ch 3 - 2 - 2 - 2 - 2 - 3, fasten off to the close-up point of Ring one.

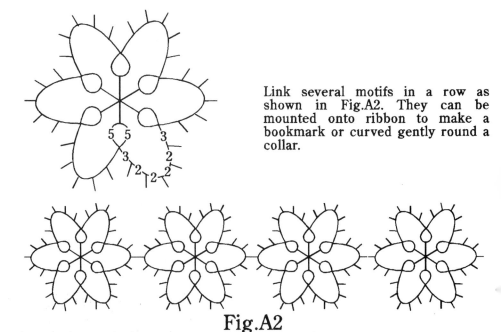

Link several motifs in a row as
shown in Fig.A2. They can be
mounted onto ribbon to make a
bookmark or curved gently round a
collar.

Fig.A2

Edelweiss

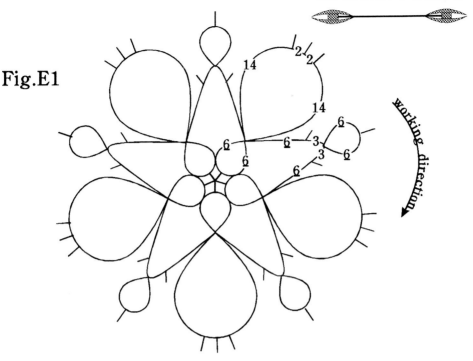

Fig.E1

working direction

Fig.E1 shows the whole motif with the first repeat numbered.

Fig.E2 shows the ds of the first repeat plus the first ring of the following repeat.
Sh1, Ring one 6 - - 6 close, RW,
Sh2, R 14 - 2 - 2 - 14 close,
Sh1, Ch 6 - 3,
Sh2, R 6 - 6 close,
Sh1, Ch 3 - 6,
repeat from the beginning 4 more times replacing Ring one with a ring which joins to it:
Sh1, R 6 + 6 close.

Fasten off to the close-up point of Ring one.

Fig.E2

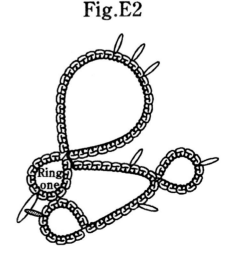

Ring one

Primrose

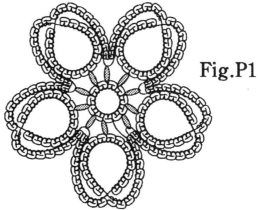

Fig.P1

Loop the thread which is between the ball and shuttle onto a safety pin, on the pin side, so that it can be released later. (Fig.P2)

Fig.P2

* Close the safety pin
Ch 10, RW,
R 8 - 8 close, RW,
Ch 10
Open the safety pin, put the picot of the ring onto the pin, then also loop the shuttle thread under the pin (Fig.P3). Repeat from * 4 more times (Fig.P4).

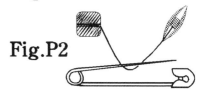

Fig.P3

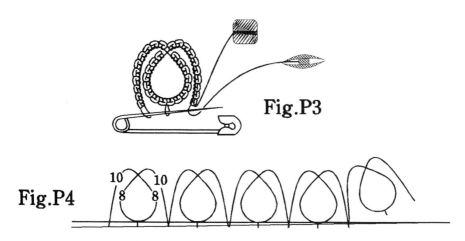

Fig.P4

Do not put the last ring and chain on the pin but reverse the work and make a ring to pick up the five loops between the chains and the five picots of the rings. Slide them one by one off the pin, making sure they are not twisted, as they are joined to a central ring (Fig.P1).
RW, R 1 + 1 + 1 + 1 + 1 + 1 + 1 + 1 + 1 + 1 close.

Daisy

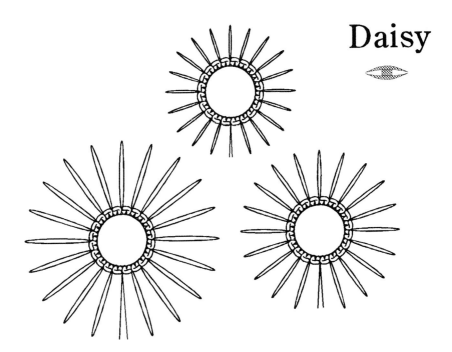

To make a daisy:
R (1 - -) 19 times 1 close, trim the two ends to the length of the picots.

Daisies can be made in assorted sizes. Make the picots with a gauge sized between 6 mm and 18 mm. More petals can be made by using two or more threads wound together on the shuttle.

Ideas and arrangements

The daisy (as well as the other flower motifs in this book) can be used in collages with embroidery or other tatting. They can be used to decorate items such as a cake frill, sewing them in place with a bead through the centre of the flower.

The arrangement shown here uses the daisy with ferns (page 20). The bowl is half of the Ring o' roses (page 12).

For other arrangements see page 14.

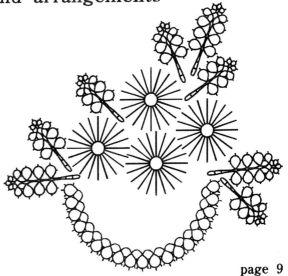

Posy

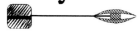

A simple ring and chain makes a small stylised flower with stem.(Figs.Y1 and Y2).

R 2 - 2 - 2 - 2 - 2 - 2 - 2 close, RW, Ch 14. Leave the ends to trim when the posy is made up.

Several of these bound together make a posy (Fig.Y3) which can then be mounted on a brooch pin or a small safety pin.

This is a way to use up thread which is left on a shuttle and is particularly effective if each flower and stem are worked in a different colour. A metre of thread is ample, half of which is wound on the shuttle. The rest is used as the ball thread.

Posy brooches are ideal to make for bazaars etc. as they don't take much time and have general appeal.

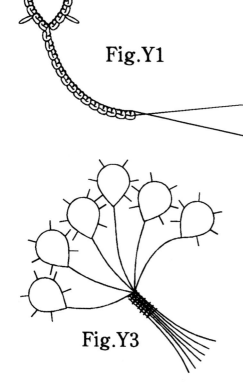

Fig.Y1

Fig.Y3

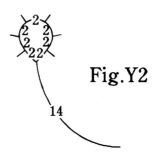

Fig.Y2

14

To make a posy

Take at least six flowers with stems. Hold them all together where the ds of the chains finish and tie them there in a tight reef knot with a separate thread. After knotting this thread lay one end with all the other stem ends and wind the other end round them all for about 1cm. Oversew to secure it then oversew this 1cm of binding to a brooch pin.

Trim the stem ends to the same length.

Viola

The Viola is worked with just one shuttle and the ball thread. Lock joins and the reverse stitch are used to get the shuttle thread into position and keep the work flat.

THE REVERSE STITCH (RS) : After working a lock join, turn the work over sideways (bringing the right hand side up and over to the left). Work the first half of a double stitch but pull it up like a single knot so that the shuttle thread changes position ready to work the next chain.

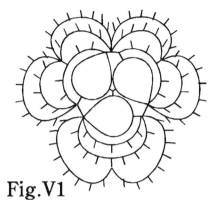

Fig.V1

Fig.V2 illustrates the bottom petal which is made first:
Ring one 5 - 5 - 10 close, RW, Ch 2 - 2 - 2 - 2 - 2 - 2, LJ to the second picot of the ring, turn the work and make a reverse stitch (explanation above) referred to in future as RS.
Ch 2 - 2 - 2 - 2 - 2 - 2 - 2 - 2 - 2 - 2, LJ to the close up point of Ring one, RS,
Ch 2 - 2 - 2 - 2 - 2 - 2 - 2 - 2 - 2, LJ to the middle picot on the previous chain,
Ch 2 - 2 - 2 - 2 - 2 - 2 - 2 - 2, LJ to Ring one at the same picot as before.

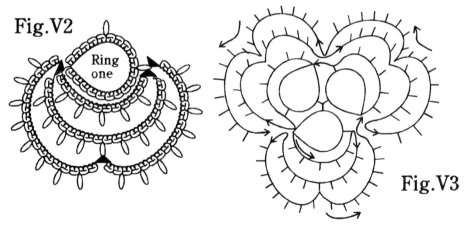

Fig.V2

Ring
one

Fig.V3

Fig.V3 shows the whole flower and the direction in which all the chains are worked. After making the lower petal (Fig.V2) complete the flower joining together the centre rings.
(RW, R 5 + 5 - 10 close, RW, Ch 2 - 2 - 2 - 2 - 2 - 2, LJ to the second picot of the last ring) twice,
LJ to the close up point of Ring one, RS,
Connect each following chain with a LJ to either a picot or to another LJ. See the positions in Figs.V1 and V3.
(Ch 2 - 2 - 2 - 2 - 2 - 2, LJ) four times, RS,
(Ch 2 - 2 - 2 - 2 - 2 - 2 - 2 - 2 - 2, LJ) four times.
Fasten off at the last LJ.

Ring o' roses

This simple little edging has a very effective use. The completed circle can attach fabric, containing a design in tatting, embroidery or needlepoint etc., to a greetings card with a circular aperture.

First make the edging to fit the pre-cut aperture in your card, so the tatting lies half way over the cut edge all round (Fig.R2).

Fig.R1

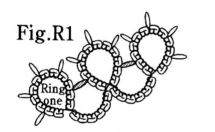

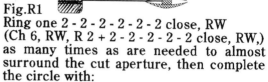

Fig.R1

Ring one 2 - 2 - 2 - 2 - 2 - 2 close, RW
(Ch 6, RW, R 2 + 2 - 2 - 2 - 2 - 2 close, RW,) as many times as are needed to almost surround the cut aperture, then complete the circle with:
Ch 6, RW, R 2 + 2 - 2 - 2 - 2 + 2 close, RW, Ch 6, fasten off to the close-up point on Ring one. Leave ends long enough to put on a needle for use when mounting.

Fig.R2

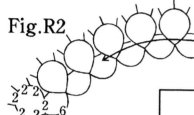

< position of cut edge of aperture

Position the fabric with design centrally behind the aperture. Place the ring of tatting on top of the card and pin it to the fabric at the top, bottom and two sides. Sew the ends of the tatting directly to the back of the fabric, then in opposite directions round the ring to be tied together when they meet. These ends come up through the fabric at the close-up point of every ring, over one thread and back through the same hole. The tatting is thus attached to the fabric and holds it in place behind the aperture.

Greetings

Jasmine

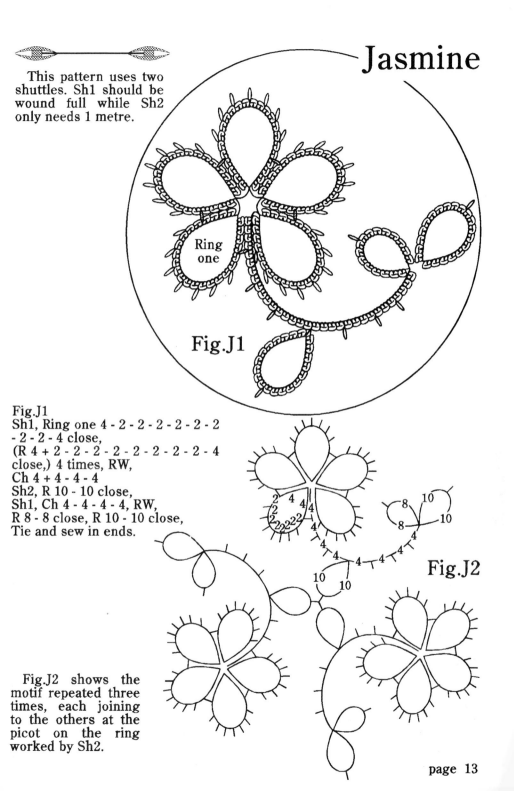

This pattern uses two shuttles. Sh1 should be wound full while Sh2 only needs 1 metre.

Ring one

Fig.J1

Fig.J1
Sh1, Ring one 4 - 2 - 2 - 2 - 2 - 2 - 2 - 2 - 2 - 4 close,
(R 4 + 2 - 2 - 2 - 2 - 2 - 2 - 2 - 2 - 4 close,) 4 times, RW,
Ch 4 + 4 - 4 - 4
Sh2, R 10 - 10 close,
Sh1, Ch 4 - 4 - 4 - 4, RW,
R 8 - 8 close, R 10 - 10 close,
Tie and sew in ends.

Fig.J2

Fig.J2 shows the motif repeated three times, each joining to the others at the picot on the ring worked by Sh2.

Arrangements

Above, Violas (page 11) and small leaves (page 21).

Below, Primroses (page 8) and long leaves (page 21).

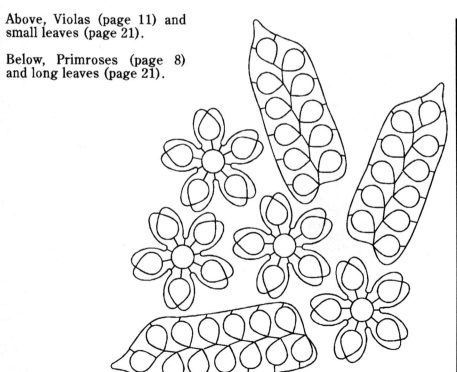

See inside back cover for key to this photograph.   page 15

Geranium

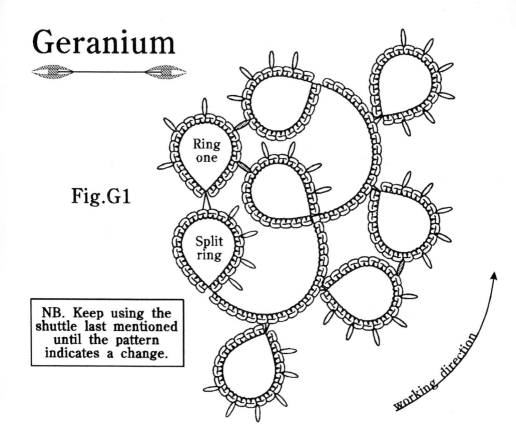

Fig.G1

Ring one

Split ring

NB. Keep using the shuttle last mentioned until the pattern indicates a change.

working direction

Both the leaf and the flower for the geranium are formed from the same pattern and are started in the same way. Fig.G1 above illustrates the start of the motif and is the leaf.

Fig.G1 THE LEAF
Sh1, Ring one 4 - 3 - 3 - 3 - 3 - 4 close.
The next ring is split. See page 3 for instructions.
Split ring Sh1, 2 - 2 - 2 - 2 - 2 Sh2, 10 close, RW,
Sh1, Ch 6, Sh2, R 8 - 2 - 2 - 2 - 2 - 2 - 2 close,
Sh1, Ch 6, Sh2, R 2 - 2 - 2 - 2 - 2 - 2 - 8 close,
Sh1, Ch 6, RW, R 10 + 2 - 2 - 2 - 2 - 2 close, * RW, Ch 6,
Sh2, R 8 + 2 - 2 - 2 - 2 - 2 - 2 close, Sh1, Ch 6,
Sh2, R 2 - 2 - 2 - 2 - 2 - 2 - 8 close,
Sh1, Ch 6, RW, R 10 + 2 - 2 - 2 - 2 - 2 close.*

Fig.G2 THE FLOWER
Work as for the leaf then repeat from * to * 3 times and finish with:
Sh1, Ch 6, Sh2, R 8 + 2 - 2 - 2 - 2 - 2 - 2 close, Sh1, Ch 6,
Sh2, R 2 - 2 - 2 - 2 - 2 - 2 + 8 close, Sh1, Ch 6.
Fasten off to the close-up point of the split ring.

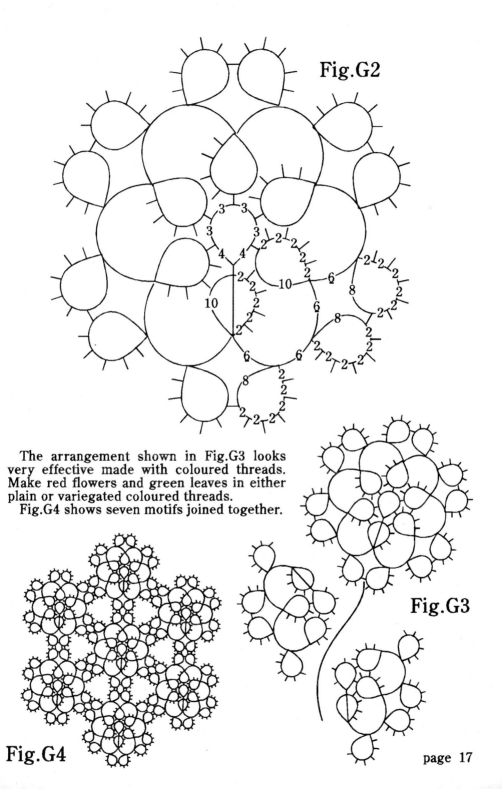

Fig.G2

The arrangement shown in Fig.G3 looks very effective made with coloured threads. Make red flowers and green leaves in either plain or variegated coloured threads.
Fig.G4 shows seven motifs joined together.

Fig.G3

Fig.G4

Clematis

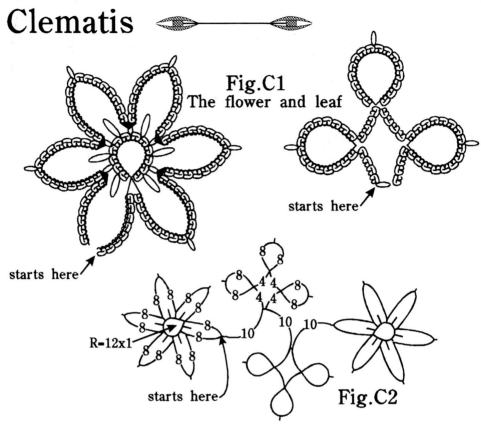

Fig.C1
The flower and leaf

starts here

starts here

R-12x1

starts here

Fig.C2

Here are the written instructions for the arrangement shown in Fig.C2.
Notice the 10ds taking the work on from flower to leaf or leaf to leaf.
Pull up all chains to give firm curves.
Remember to change shuttles only when the pattern dictates.
The flower begins with a chain, held at the start on a paperclip or safety pin
(see Fig.P2 on page 8).
Sh1 Ch 8, RW, The next ring is the centre of the flower and has alternate
long and short picots.
R 1 - - 1 - 1 - - 1 - 1 - - 1 - 1 - - 1 - 1 - - 1 - 1 - - 1 close, RW,
(Ch 8 - 8, LJ to the next short picot of the ring,) 5 times,
Ch 8 LJ to the starting picot on the paperclip.
Ch 10 - 4, RW, R 8 - 8 close, RW,
(Ch 4, RW, R 8 - 8 close, RW,) twice,
Ch 4, RW,
Sh2, LJ to adjacent free picot, Ch 10 - 4, RW,
(R 8 - 8 close, RW, Ch 4, RW,) twice,
R 8 - 8 close, RW, Ch 4 + 10, loop a paperclip over Sh2 thread and continue
the same chain which begins another flower, Ch 8, RW, R 1 - - 1 - 1 - - 1 - 1 - -
1 - 1 - - 1 - 1 - - 1 - 1 - - 1 close,
(Ch 8 - 8, LJ to the next short picot or the ring,) 5 times,
Ch 8. Fasten off to the thread held on the paperclip.

The clematis sprig in Fig.C2 would be suitable for an oval mount. The experienced tatter could work the asymmetrical design in Fig.C3 by connecting the same flowers and leaves with the stems and buds as marked. Two shuttles would be used to make the chains curve in the right direction. This, or your own asymmetrical creation, could accompany embroidery or be part of a collage with other tatting.

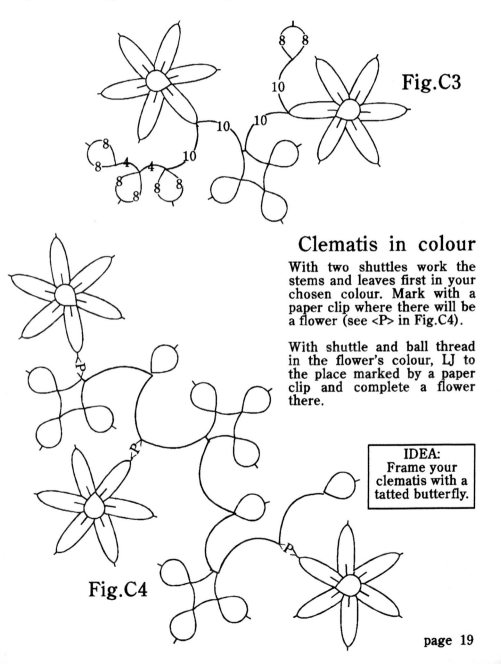

Fig.C3

Clematis in colour

With two shuttles work the stems and leaves first in your chosen colour. Mark with a paper clip where there will be a flower (see <P> in Fig.C4).

With shuttle and ball thread in the flower's colour, LJ to the place marked by a paper clip and complete a flower there.

> IDEA:
> Frame your clematis with a tatted butterfly.

Fig.C4

Fern

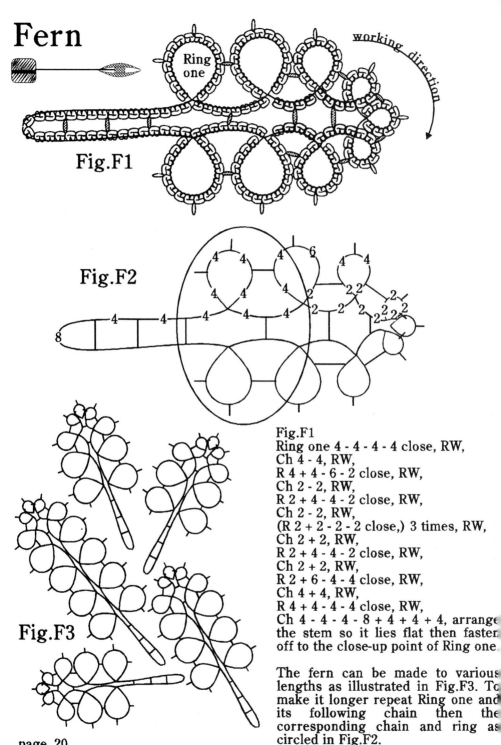

Ring one

working direction

Fig.F1

Fig.F2

Fig.F3

Fig.F1
Ring one 4 - 4 - 4 - 4 close, RW,
Ch 4 - 4, RW,
R 4 + 4 - 6 - 2 close, RW,
Ch 2 - 2, RW,
R 2 + 4 - 4 - 2 close, RW,
Ch 2 - 2, RW,
(R 2 + 2 - 2 - 2 close,) 3 times, RW,
Ch 2 + 2, RW,
R 2 + 4 - 4 - 2 close, RW,
Ch 2 + 2, RW,
R 2 + 6 - 4 - 4 close, RW,
Ch 4 + 4, RW,
R 4 + 4 - 4 - 4 close, RW,
Ch 4 - 4 - 4 - 8 + 4 + 4 + 4, arrange
the stem so it lies flat then fasten
off to the close-up point of Ring one.

The fern can be made to various
lengths as illustrated in Fig.F3. To
make it longer repeat Ring one and
its following chain then the
corresponding chain and ring as
circled in Fig.F2.

Leaf

NB. The leaf will be constantly turned over in the making. Fig.L1 is the correct way round for Ring one but is back to front at the end. In illustrating the leaf here spaces have occurred between the ds. In actual fact, work the chains close to the rings down the centre then ease the outside chain to fit.

Fig.L1

Fig.L1
Sh1, Ring one 4 - 4 - 4 close,
*Sh2, Ch 2,
Sh1, R 6 - 6 close, RW, Ch 2,
Sh2, R 6 - 6 close, RW, (omit RW on the last repeat)
repeat from * for the length required.
(Fig.L1 has one repeat)
Place a marker thread over Sh1 thread, next to the last ring worked.
Sh1 now works an inward facing chain all the way round the outside of the leaf.
Sh1, Ch8 + , join to the picot on the last ring worked.
**Ch 8 + , join to the picot on the next ring up on that same side.
Repeat from ** to the side picot on Ring one.
To make the tip of the leaf, the chain is joined to itself:
Ch 4 - 4 + 4 + (join to the other side picot of Ring one.)
*** Ch 8 + join to the picot on the next ring down the other side.
Repeat from *** til the last ring is connected.
Ch 8 + remove the marker and join there.
Ch 8 for a stalk, then tie the two ends together in a single knot and trim close.
Fasten off to the marked point for no stalk.

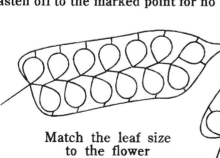

Match the leaf size
to the flower
or arrangement

Ivy

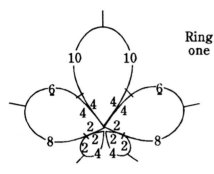

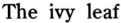

Ring one

The ivy leaf

*Ring one 4 - 2 - 2 close,
R 2 + 8 - 6 - 4 close,
R 4 + 10 - 10 - 4 close,
R 4 + 6 - 8 - 2 close,
R 2 + 2 - 4 close, RW,
Ch 50 half stitches to make a spiral stem.
Tie the two ends together in a single knot and trim.*

To make a runner of several leaves and stems repeat from * to *, as many times as required, without breaking the thread.

Spiral stem

Make a chain with purl stitches only, i.e. the second half of the ds. Every ten half stitches pause to twist the work completed so far round the shuttle thread in use.

Shamrock

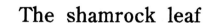

Ring one

The shamrock leaf

The rings in this leaf all have the
same number of ds so close them to
be identical in size.
Ring one 14 - 6 close,
R 6 + 12 - 2 close,
R 2 + 12 - 6 close,
R 6 + 12 - 2 close,
R 2 + 12 - 6 close,
R 6 + 14 close, RW,
Ch (5 times the first half of ds then
5 times the second half of ds) 5 times.
Tie the ends together in a single knot
and trim.

Ric-rac stem

Make a chain with five
plain stitches (the first
half of the ds) then
five purl stitches (the
second half of the ds)
and repeat for the
length required. The
two sets of stitches
will lie to opposite
sides of the shuttle
thread on which they
were made.

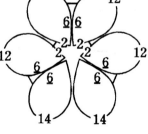

IDEA:
Make a shamrock
brooch in the same
way as the posy on
page 10

Clover

The clover leaf or trefoil is often used in tatting and consists of three rings worked one after the other. This pattern is a runner of four clover leaves which get bigger and bigger, separated by chains which also get progressively bigger. It can be repeated to make a scalloped edging (Fig.CV3).

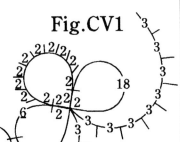

Fig.CV1

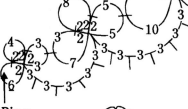

Ring one

Fig.CV2

Fig.CV1 is a diagram of the whole runner.
Fig.CV2 shows details of the stitches at the beginning.
Ring one 6 - 2 close, R 2 + 4 - 2 close, R 2 + 3 - 3 close, RW,
Ch 3 - 3 - 3 - 3 - 3, RW,
R 7 + 3 - 2 close, R 2 + 8 - 2 close, R 2 + 5 - 5 close, RW,
Ch 3 - 3 - 3 - 3 - 3 - 3, RW,
R 10 + 4 - 2 close, R 2 + 12 - 2 close, R 2 + 6 - 8 close, RW,
Ch 3 - 3 - 3 - 3 - 3 - 3 - 3, RW,
R 12 + 6 - 2 close, R 2 + 2 - 2 - 2 - 2 - 2 - 2 - 2 - 2 - 2 - 2 - 2 close,
R 2 + 18 close, RW,
Ch 3 - 3 - 3 - 3 - 3 - 3 - 3 - 3.
Fasten off here for one runner. If the edging is being made, RW and start again at Ring one.

Fig.CV3

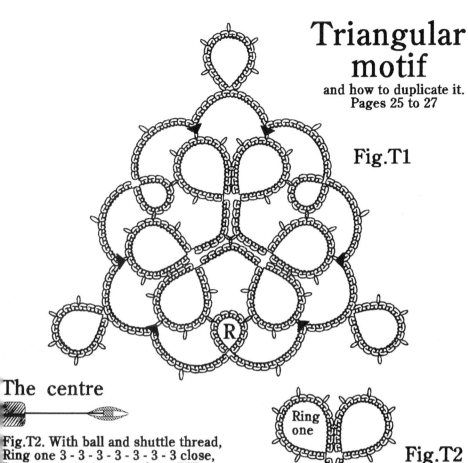

Triangular motif
and how to duplicate it.
Pages 25 to 27

Fig.T1

The centre

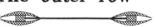

Fig.T2. With ball and shuttle thread,
Ring one 3 - 3 - 3 - 3 - 3 - 3 - 3 close,
R 3 + 3 - 3 - 3 - 3 - 3 - 3 close, RW,
Ch 4 - 4, RW,
*R 3 - 3 - 3 - 3 - 3 - 3 - 3 close,
R 3 + 3 - 3 - 3 - 3 - 3 - 3 close, RW,
Ch 4 + 4, RW,
Repeat from * once more.
Fasten off to the close-up point of
Ring one.

Fig.T2

Ring one

The outer row

With two shuttles start with the ring marked R in Fig.T1 and follow the
diagram round to see where the joins are made.
* Sh1, R 4 + 4 + 4 close, RW,
Ch 6 - 6 , LJ, Ch 6
Sh2, R 3 - 3 - 3 - 3 - 3 - 3 close
Sh1, Ch 6, LJ, Ch 6 - 6
Repeat from * two more times.
Fasten off to the close-up point of the first ring of this round.

page 25

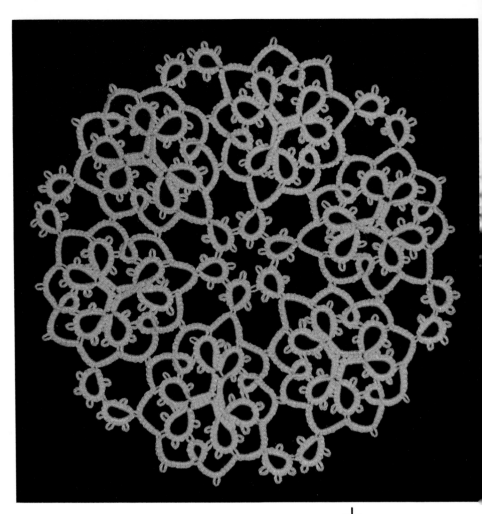

The photograph above illustrates a coaster made with six of these triangular motifs which have been joined together.

Fig.T3 shows one triangular motif in line form. On page 27 four of these motifs are shown together so the worker can see where to make the joins.

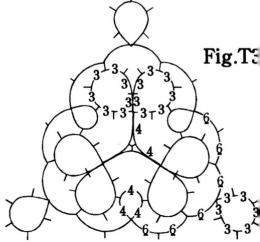

Fig.T3

The symbol ⊕ in Fig.T4 shows were one motif is joined onto the picots of another motif.

Fig.T4

Fig.T4 shows that a larger triangle is formed when four small triangles are joined thus:

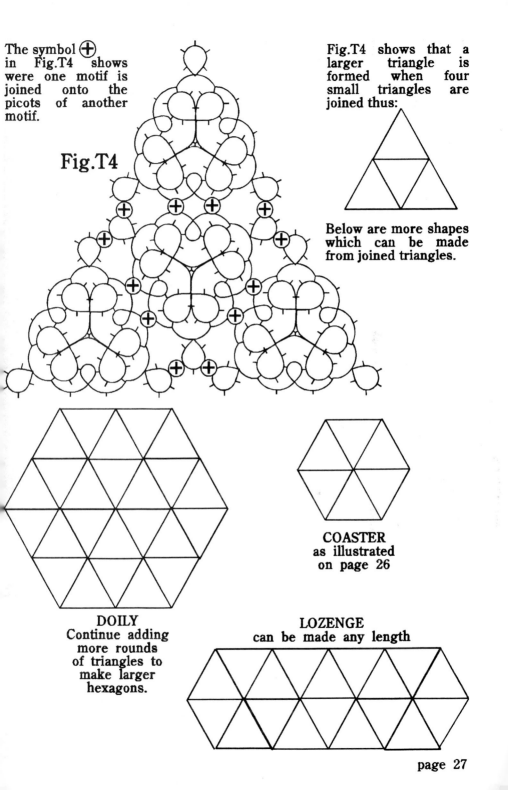

Below are more shapes which can be made from joined triangles.

COASTER
as illustrated
on page 26

DOILY
Continue adding
more rounds
of triangles to
make larger
hexagons.

LOZENGE
can be made any length

Queen Anne's Lace

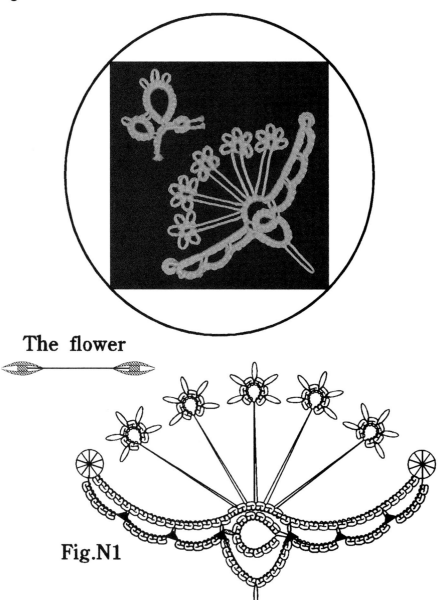

The flower

Fig.N1

The flower is worked all in one. Start from the josephine knot on the left hand side, work along the top of the flower to the josephine knot on the right, then back again underneath the flower. The written instructions are at the top of the next page.

Fig.N2

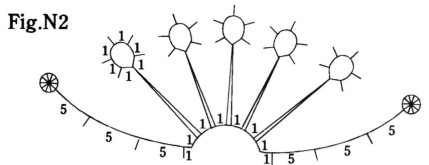

Fig.N2 Sh1, JK 10, RW, Ch 5 - 5 - 5 - 1, RW,
(Sh2, Ch 1, leave 1cm of Sh1 thread,
Sh1, R 1 - 1 - 1 - 1 - 1 - 1 close, leave 1cm of Sh1 thread,) 5 times,
Sh2, Ch 1, RW,
Sh1, Ch 1 - 5 - 5 - 5, RW, JK 10

Fig.N3 Sh2, (Ch 5, LJ to the next picot on the adjacent chain,) 3 times,
RW, R 6 + 6 close, RW, Ch 6 - - 6, LJ, 5, LJ, 5, LJ, 5,
Finish off to the close-up point of the first JK.

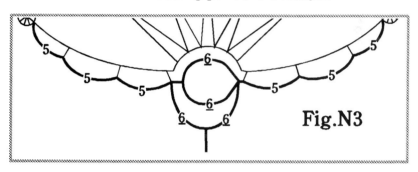

Fig.N3

Fig.N4

Ring one

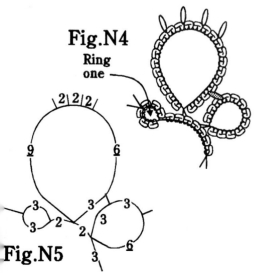

The butterfly

Figs.N4 and N5
Sh1, Ring one, 3 - - 3 close,
RW, Ch 2,
Sh2, R 9 - 2 - 2 - 2 - 6 - 3 close,
Sh1, Ch 2
Sh2, R 3 + 3 - 6 close
Sh1, Ch 3, Tie tail ends
together in a single knot and
trim.
Cut the picot in Ring one to
make antennae.

Fig.N5

BOW - for dress, hair or bouquet

This bow is worked in three sections: the centre (Fig.B1) and two sides. Fig.B3 shows where one side joins to the centre. Both sides are the same and are each worked in one piece. Follow the instructions below for the centre and Fig.B4 for the sides with written instructions on page 32.

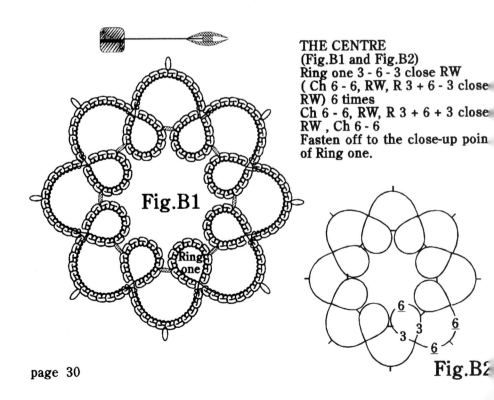

Fig.B1

Ring one

THE CENTRE
(Fig.B1 and Fig.B2)
Ring one 3 - 6 - 3 close RW
(Ch 6 - 6, RW, R 3 + 6 - 3 close RW) 6 times
Ch 6 - 6, RW, R 3 + 6 + 3 close RW , Ch 6 - 6
Fasten off to the close-up poin of Ring one.

Fig.B2

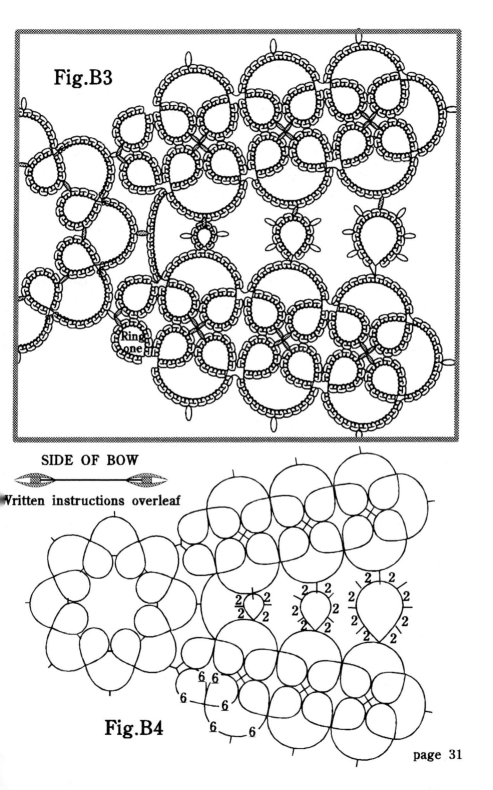

Fig.B3

SIDE OF BOW

Written instructions overleaf

Ring one

Fig.B4

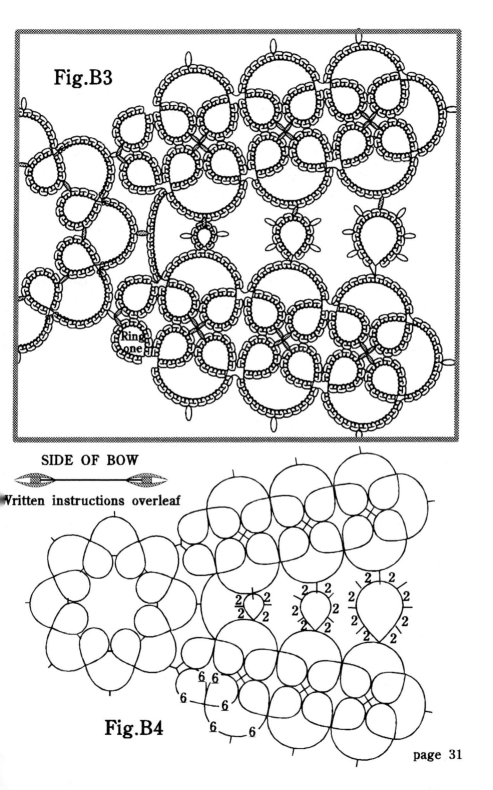

THE SIDE - With two shuttles;
Sh1, Ring one 6 + 6 close,
(R 6 - 6 close, RW, Ch 6 - 6, RW R 6 + 6 close) 3 times.
RW, Ch 6 - 6, RW, R 6 + 6 close, Ch 6
Sh2, R 2 - 2 - 2 - 2 - 2 - 2 - 2 - 2 close,
Sh1, Ch 6, RW, (R 6 + 6 close) twice, RW, Ch 6,
Sh2, R 2 - 2 - 2 - 2 - 2 - 2 close,
Sh1, Ch 6, RW, (R 6 + 6 close) twice, RW, Ch 6,
Sh2, R 2 - 2 - 2 - 2 close,
Sh1, Ch 6, RW, (R 6 + 6 close) twice,
Sh2, Ch 6 + 6,
Sh1, R 6 + 6 close (R 6 - 6 close, RW, Ch 6 + 6, RW, R 6 + 6 close) 3 times.
RW, Ch 6 - 6, RW, R 6 + 6 close,
[(R 6 + 6 close,) twice, RW, Ch 6 - 6, RW] 3 times
Cut and tie ends and sew in.
Make the other side the same remembering to leave free a top and bottom
chain of the centre (see Fig.B5)

NB. Keep using the
shuttle last mentioned
until the pattern
indicates a change.

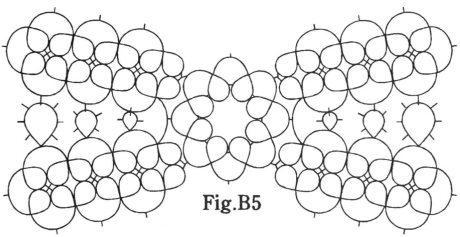

Fig.B5

If you would like the bow to be narrower, adapt the pattern as illustrated in
Fig.B6. The sides are worked in the same manner but have several rings and
chains missing from the ends.

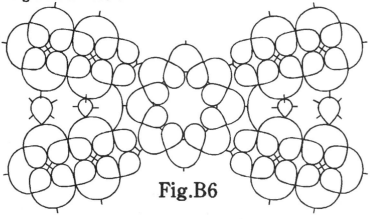

Fig.B6